This book belongs to:

____

____

____

Copyright © 2020 by Dan Siam

Table of Contents

Table of Contents

Recipes

Page

Table of Contents

 Table of Contents

Ingredients

Rating

☆☆☆☆☆

Difficulty

○○○○○

Serves

1 2 3 4 ......

Cooking Time

Directions

Best Served With

Notes

Ingredients

Rating

Difficulty

Serves
1 2 3 4 ......

Cooking Time

Directions

Best Served With

Notes

....
Ingredients

Rating
☆☆☆☆☆

Difficulty
◯ ◯ ◯ ◯ ◯

Serves
1 2 3 4 ......

Cooking Time

Directions

Best Served With

Notes

Ingredients

Rating
☆☆☆☆☆

Difficulty
○ ○ ○ ○ ○

Serves
1 2 3 4 ......

Cooking Time

Directions

Best Served With

Notes

....

Ingredients

Rating
☆ ☆ ☆ ☆ ☆

Difficulty
○ ○ ○ ○ ○

Serves
1 2 3 4 ......

Cooking Time

Directions

Best Served With

Notes

11

....

Ingredients

Rating

☆ ☆ ☆ ☆

Difficulty

○ ○ ○ ○ ○

Serves

1 2 3 4 ......

Cooking Time

Directions

Best Served With

Notes

Ingredients

Rating

Difficulty

Serves

1 2 3 4 ......

Cooking Time

Best Served With

Directions

Notes

....

Ingredients

Directions

Ingredients

Directions

Rating

Difficulty

Serves

1 2 3 4 ......

Cooking Time

Best Served With

Notes

15

Ingredients

Directions

Rating

Difficulty

Serves

1 2 3 4 ......

Cooking Time

Best Served With

Notes

Ingredients

Directions

Rating

Difficulty

Serves

1 2 3 4 ......

Cooking Time

Best Served With

Notes

Ingredients

Rating

Difficulty

Serves
1 2 3 4 ......

Cooking Time

Directions

Best Served With

Notes

18

....
Ingredients

Rating
☆ ☆ ☆ ☆ ☆

Difficulty
○ ○ ○ ○ ○

Serves
1 2 3 4 ......

Cooking Time

Directions

Best Served With

Notes

....
Ingredients

Difficulty

Serves

1 2 3 4 ......

Cooking Time

Directions

Best Served With

Notes

Ingredients

Rating
☆☆☆☆☆

Difficulty
○ ○ ○ ○ ○

Serves
1 2 3 4 ......

Cooking Time

Best Served With

Directions

Notes

21

Ingredients

Rating

Difficulty

Serves

1 2 3 4 ......

Cooking Time

Directions

Best Served With

Notes

Ingredients

Directions

Ingredients

Rating

Difficulty

Serves

1 2 3 4 ......

Cooking Time

Directions

Best Served With

Notes

Ingredients

Directions

Rating
☆☆☆☆☆

Difficulty
○ ○ ○ ○ ○

Serves
1 2 3 4 ......

Cooking Time

Best Served With

Notes

Ingredients

Directions

Rating

Difficulty

Serves

1 2 3 4 ......

Cooking Time

Best Served With

Notes

Ingredients

Directions

Rating

Difficulty

Serves
1 2 3 4 ......

Cooking Time

Best Served With

Notes

27

....

Ingredients

Directions

Rating

Difficulty

Serves

1 2 3 4 ......

Cooking Time

Best Served With

Notes

Ingredients

Directions

Rating

Difficulty

Serves

1 2 3 4 ......

Cooking Time

Best Served With

Notes

Ingredients

Directions

Rating

Difficulty

Serves

1 2 3 4 ......

Cooking Time

Best Served With

Notes

Ingredients

Rating

Difficulty

Serves

1 2 3 4 ......

Cooking Time

Directions

Best Served With

Notes

Ingredients

Directions

Rating

Difficulty

Serves
1 2 3 4 ......

Cooking Time

Best Served With

Notes

Ingredients

Rating

Difficulty

○ ○ ○ ○ ○

Serves

1 2 3 4 ......

Cooking Time

Best Served With

Notes

Directions

33

Ingredients

Rating
☆☆☆☆☆

Difficulty
○ ○ ○ ○ ○

Serves
1 2 3 4 ......

Cooking Time

Directions

Best Served With

Notes

34

....

Ingredients

Rating
☆☆☆☆☆

Difficulty
○○○○○

Serves
1 2 3 4 ......

Cooking Time

Directions

Best Served With

Notes

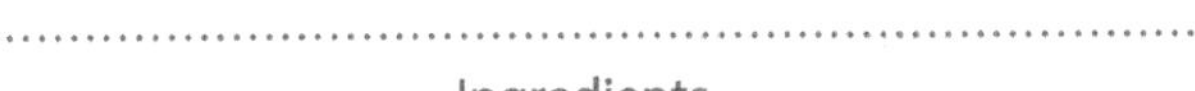

Ingredients

Rating

Difficulty

Serves
1 2 3 4 ......

Cooking Time

Directions

Best Served With

Notes

Ingredients

Rating

Difficulty

Serves

1 2 3 4 ......

Cooking Time

Best Served With

Directions

Notes

37

Ingredients

Rating

Difficulty

Serves

1 2 3 4 ......

Cooking Time

Best Served With

Directions

Notes

38

Ingredients

Rating

Difficulty

Serves

1 2 3 4 ......

Cooking Time

Directions

Best Served With

Notes

....

Ingredients

Directions

Rating

Difficulty

Serves
1 2 3 4 ......

Cooking Time

Best Served With

Notes

Ingredients

Directions

Rating

Difficulty

Serves

1 2 3 4 ......

Cooking Time

Best Served With

Notes

Ingredients

Rating

☆☆☆☆☆

Difficulty

○ ○ ○ ○ ○

Serves

1 2 3 4 ......

Cooking Time

Directions

Best Served With

Notes

Ingredients

Rating

Difficulty

Serves
1 2 3 4 ......

Cooking Time

Directions

Best Served With

Notes

43

Ingredients

Directions

Rating

Difficulty

Serves
1 2 3 4 ......

Cooking Time

Best Served With

Notes

Ingredients

Rating
☆☆☆☆☆

Difficulty
○ ○ ○ ○ ○

Serves
1 2 3 4 ......

Cooking Time

Best Served With

Directions

Notes

Ingredients

Rating
☆☆☆☆☆

Difficulty
○○○○○

Serves
1 2 3 4 ......

Cooking Time

Directions

Best Served With

Notes

....

Ingredients

Rating
☆ ☆ ☆ ☆ ☆

Difficulty
○ ○ ○ ○ ○

Serves
1 2 3 4 ......

Cooking Time

Directions

Best Served With

Notes

47

Ingredients

Rating

Difficulty

○ ○ ○ ○ ○

Serves

1 2 3 4 ......

Cooking Time

Directions

Best Served With

Notes

Ingredients

Rating

Difficulty

Serves
1 2 3 4 ......

Cooking Time

Best Served With

Directions

Notes

49

Ingredients

Rating

☆☆☆☆☆

Difficulty

○○○○○

Serves

1 2 3 4 ......

Cooking Time

Best Served With

Directions

Notes

Ingredients

Rating

Difficulty

Serves

1 2 3 4 ......

Cooking Time

Directions

Best Served With

Notes

51

....

Ingredients

Rating

☆☆☆☆☆

Difficulty

○○○○○

Serves

1 2 3 4 ......

Cooking Time

Directions

Best Served With

Notes

Ingredients

Directions

Rating

Difficulty

Serves

1 2 3 4 ......

Cooking Time

Best Served With

Notes

Ingredients

Rating

Difficulty

Serves
1 2 3 4 ......

Cooking Time

Directions

Best Served With

Notes

Ingredients

Rating

Difficulty

Serves

1 2 3 4 ......

Cooking Time

Directions

Best Served With

Notes

....

Ingredients

Rating

Difficulty

Serves

1 2 3 4 ......

Cooking Time

Directions

Best Served With

Notes

56

Ingredients

Rating
☆☆☆☆☆

Difficulty
○ ○ ○ ○ ○

Serves
1 2 3 4 ......

Cooking Time

Directions

Best Served With

Notes

Ingredients

Rating

Difficulty

Serves

1 2 3 4 ......

Cooking Time

Best Served With

Directions

Notes

....

Ingredients

Rating
☆ ☆ ☆ ☆

Difficulty
○ ○ ○ ○ ○

Serves
1 2 3 4 ......

Cooking Time

Directions

Best Served With

Notes

59

....
Ingredients

Rating
☆ ☆ ☆ ☆ ☆

Difficulty
○ ○ ○ ○ ○

Serves
1 2 3 4 ......

Cooking Time

Directions

Best Served With

Notes

Ingredients

Rating

Difficulty

Serves

1 2 3 4 ......

Cooking Time

Best Served With

Directions

Notes

Ingredients

Rating

Difficulty

Serves
1 2 3 4 ......

Cooking Time

Directions

Best Served With

Notes

....

Ingredients

Rating

Difficulty

Serves

1 2 3 4 ......

Cooking Time

Directions

Best Served With

Notes

....

Ingredients

Rating

Difficulty

○ ○ ○ ○ ○

Serves

1 2 3 4 ......

Cooking Time

Directions

Best Served With

Notes

64

Ingredients

Directions

Rating

Difficulty

Serves

1 2 3 4 ......

Cooking Time

Best Served With

Notes

....

Ingredients

Directions

Rating
☆☆☆☆☆

Difficulty
○○○○○

Serves
1 2 3 4 ......

Cooking Time

Best Served With

Notes

66

....

Ingredients

Rating
☆ ☆ ☆ ☆

Difficulty
○ ○ ○ ○ ○

Serves
1 2 3 4 ......

Cooking Time

Best Served With

Directions

Notes

67

Ingredients

Directions

Rating
☆☆☆☆☆

Difficulty
○○○○○

Serves
1 2 3 4 ......

Cooking Time

Best Served With

Notes

68

Ingredients

Rating

Difficulty

Serves

1 2 3 4 ......

Cooking Time

Best Served With

Notes

Directions

....

Ingredients

Rating
☆ ☆ ☆ ☆ ☆

Difficulty
○ ○ ○ ○ ○

Serves
1 2 3 4 ......

Cooking Time

Directions

Best Served With

Notes

70

Ingredients

Directions

Rating

☆☆☆☆☆

Difficulty

○○○○○

Serves

1 2 3 4 ......

Cooking Time

Best Served With

Notes

Ingredients

Directions

Rating

Difficulty

Serves

1 2 3 4 ......

Cooking Time

Best Served With

Notes

Ingredients

Rating

Difficulty

Serves

1 2 3 4 ......

Cooking Time

Directions

Best Served With

Notes

....

Ingredients

Rating

☆ ☆ ☆ ☆ ☆

Difficulty

○ ○ ○ ○ ○

Serves

1 2 3 4 ......

Cooking Time

Directions

Best Served With

Notes

Ingredients

Rating

Difficulty

Serves

1 2 3 4 ......

Cooking Time

Directions

Best Served With

Notes

Ingredients

Directions

Rating

Difficulty

Serves

1 2 3 4 ......

Cooking Time

Best Served With

Notes

76

Ingredients

Rating

Difficulty

Serves

1 2 3 4 ......

Cooking Time

Directions

Best Served With

Notes

Ingredients

Directions

Difficulty

Serves

1 2 3 4 ......

Cooking Time

Best Served With

Notes

Ingredients

Directions

Rating

Difficulty

Serves
1 2 3 4 ......

Cooking Time

Best Served With

Notes

Ingredients

Rating

Difficulty

Serves

1 2 3 4 ......

Cooking Time

Directions

Best Served With

Notes

Ingredients

Rating

Difficulty

Serves

1 2 3 4 ......

Cooking Time

Directions

Best Served With

Notes

Ingredients

Rating

☆ ☆ ☆ ☆ ☆

Difficulty

○ ○ ○ ○ ○

Serves

1 2 3 4 ......

Cooking Time

Directions

Best Served With

Notes

....

Ingredients

Rating
☆ ☆ ☆ ☆ ☆

Difficulty
○ ○ ○ ○ ○

Serves
1 2 3 4 ......

Cooking Time

Directions

Best Served With

Notes

Ingredients

Rating

Difficulty

Serves

1 2 3 4 ......

Cooking Time

Directions

Best Served With

Notes

84

Ingredients

Rating

☆☆☆☆☆

Difficulty

○ ○ ○ ○ ○

Serves

1 2 3 4 ......

Cooking Time

Directions

Best Served With

Notes

Ingredients

Directions

Rating

☆ ☆ ☆ ☆ ☆

Difficulty
○ ○ ○ ○ ○

Serves
1 2 3 4 ......

Cooking Time

Best Served With

Notes

Ingredients

Rating
☆☆☆☆☆

Difficulty
○○○○○

Serves
1 2 3 4 ......

Cooking Time

Directions

Best Served With

Notes

....

Ingredients

Directions

Rating

Difficulty

Serves

1 2 3 4 ......

Cooking Time

Best Served With

Notes

Ingredients

Rating

Difficulty

Serves

1 2 3 4 ......

Cooking Time

Directions

Best Served With

Notes

89

Ingredients

Rating

Difficulty

Serves

1 2 3 4 ......

Cooking Time

Directions

Best Served With

Notes

....

Ingredients

Directions

Rating

Difficulty

Serves

1 2 3 4 ......

Cooking Time

Best Served With

Notes

....

Ingredients

Rating

☆☆☆☆☆

Difficulty

○ ○ ○ ○ ○

Serves

1 2 3 4 ......

Cooking Time

Directions

Best Served With

Notes

92

Ingredients

Directions

Rating

☆ ☆ ☆ ☆

Difficulty

○ ○ ○ ○ ○

Serves

1 2 3 4 ......

Cooking Time

Best Served With

Notes

Ingredients

Directions

Rating

Difficulty

Serves

1 2 3 4 ......

Cooking Time

Best Served With

Notes

Ingredients

Rating

Difficulty

Serves
1 2 3 4 ......

Cooking Time

Directions

Best Served With

Notes

95

....

Ingredients

Rating
☆☆☆☆☆

Difficulty
○○○○○

Serves
1 2 3 4 ......

Cooking Time

Directions

Best Served With

Notes

....
Ingredients

Rating
☆☆☆☆☆

Difficulty
○ ○ ○ ○ ○

Serves
1 2 3 4 ......

Cooking Time

Directions

Best Served With

Notes

Ingredients

Rating
☆☆☆☆☆

Difficulty
○○○○○

Serves
1 2 3 4 ......

Cooking Time

Directions

Best Served With

Notes

98

....

Ingredients

Directions

Rating

☆☆☆☆☆

Difficulty

○○○○○

Serves

1 2 3 4 ......

Cooking Time

Best Served With

Notes

99

Ingredients

Rating
☆☆☆☆☆

Difficulty
○○○○○

Serves
1 2 3 4 ......

Cooking Time

Directions

Best Served With

Notes

Ingredients

Directions

Rating

Difficulty

Serves

1 2 3 4 ......

Cooking Time

Best Served With

Notes